How Newspapers Are Made

Text   Sarah Waters
Design Eddie Poulton

Contents

page 2 All Kinds of Newspapers
        4 History
        6 Who Makes a Newspaper?
        8 Front Page Story
     10 The Editor
     12 The Reporter
     14 The Pictures Editor
     16 The Specialist
     18 The Design Department
     20 The Copy-Editor
     22 Page Make-up
     24 Processing
     26 Printing and Publishing
     28 Distribution and Sales
     30 Facts and Figures
     31 Glossary
     32 Index and Acknowledgments

Facts On File
New York • Oxford

All Kinds of Newspapers

Newspapers were founded to bring the news to the people. As well as providing general information they also bring particular kinds of news to particular people. Whatever your taste and interests you can find a newspaper to suit you. You can take *The International Herald Tribune* for a world's eye view or *The Wichinaga Gazette* to find out what has been happening in your neighborhood.

As well as news, the paper will have what are known as "features": stories of general interest; gossip columns; theater, cinema and television reviews and programs; sporting pages; fashion pages; and background articles on subjects which are in the news. In the words of John Walter, the founder of *The Times* of London: "A News-paper ought to be the Register of the Times and faithful recorder of every species of

Left. Newspapers of many kinds from all over the world are displayed on this news-stand in the Canary Islands.

Opposite. Two newspapers produced for two different types of readership. (Left) The *New York Times*, a world-famous paper with a daily circulation of over one million. On Sundays, with all its supplements, it is the heaviest newspaper in the world. (Right) The *Garavi Gujarat*, founded in 1968 for the growing Gujarati Indian community in Britain. It appears weekly and has a circulation of 45,000.

intelligence; it ought not to be engrossed by any particular object but, like a well-covered table, it should contain something suited to every palate."

Some newspapers are of a large, broadsheet size, suitable for serious, leisurely reading. Some are of small, tabloid size, with lots of short, snappy items, geared for quick scanning and useful for rush-hour travel. Some appear daily, some once a week. Some have ten sections. Others consist of a single folded sheet. Some have full-color pictures. Others have no pictures at all.

Newspapers have an advantage over radio and television as a means of providing information. You can select what you want to read. Instead of having to watch or listen to a whole bulletin—as with TV or radio—you can pick and choose the parts of the paper that interest you. If spoken on radio the eight columns of a broadsheet page would last about an hour; they would take two, three or four times longer on television, with pictures to watch as well.

Newspapers provide a record of daily happenings. You can cut out an item that interests you, or you can check on facts—the winner of a race or a tennis match. If you would like to know what was happening in the year when you were born, you can look up a newspaper in your library.

In the United States, most newspapers are based on a city, and cover the area around it. They carry national and international news geared to their own region. Among such famous papers are *The New York Times, The Los Angeles Times, The Boston Herald* and *The Boston Globe.*

The British are great newspaper readers—with twelve national dailies, eight national Sunday papers and a flourishing local press. In France there is a mixture of national and local papers. Germany has newspapers which circulate in several regions with different additions to the basic framework for the different regions. Japan has two national newspapers with huge circulations, *The Yomiuri Shimbun* and *The Asahi Shimbun,* as well as many others.

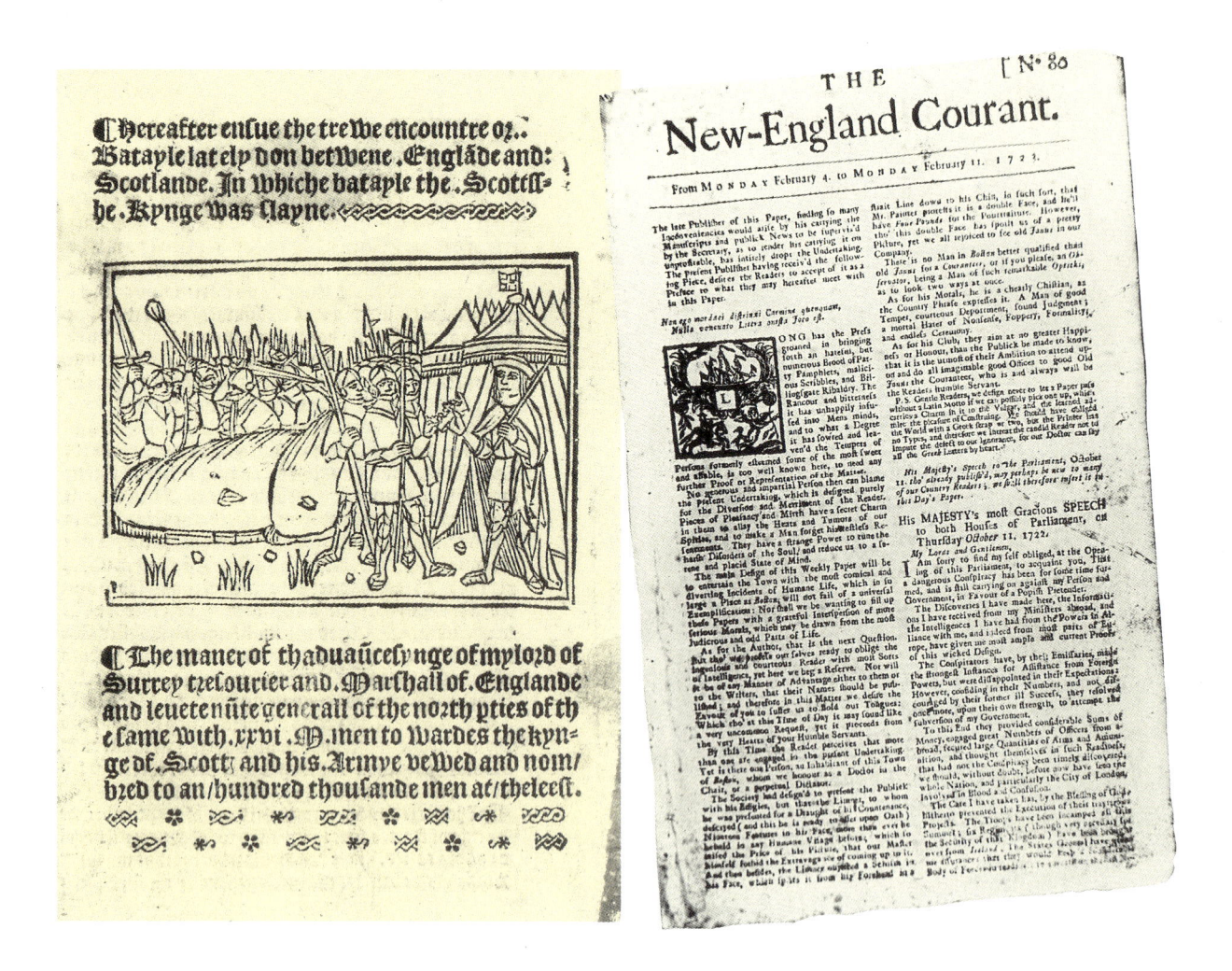

History

Left. Front page news in 1513: the Battle of Flodden, from the first illustrated English news pamphlet. Right. The *New England Courant*, on which Benjamin Franklin began his newspaper career as an apprentice to his brother.

Occasional news-sheets were first printed in the 16th Century, describing a single, sensational event. By the early 17th Century they were beginning to appear more frequently in Europe, and in 1620 the first regular news-book, made of folded news-sheets, was published in English. It was the *Weekly Newes from Italy, Germanie, Hungary*, translated from a Dutch original. The idea of a regular series appealed to the public, and others followed. They were called *courants* or *corantos*.

Before printing was invented, news had been circulated by news-letters. Some were written to provide information for a particular person, business or community. Others were copied out by professional scribes under the direction of a **news-monger**, and were distributed to paying customers. It was from these beginnings that Fleet Street became the center of British newspapers. In the 17th Century the nave of St Paul's Cathedral in London was the place where news-mongers gathered to exchange the news of the day: the letter-writers therefore set up their offices in neighboring Fleet Street and the area around it.

News-letters continued to be published for some time after the arrival of newspapers. John Campbell, the postmaster of Boston, Massachussetts, combined the two. For several years he supplied news-letters to the colonial governors of New England. Then on April 9, 1704, he published *The Boston News-Letter*: the first American newspaper. It ran until the Declaration of Independence in 1776.

In England the first daily paper, *The Daily Courant*, had been published as far back as 1702. Originally it was printed on one side only of a small sheet, but it was soon expanded to four sheets, and more than one edition was produced in the course of a day. It closed down in 1735.

At this period famous authors began to be associated with the press. Daniel Defoe, Jonathan Swift and Henry Fielding all edited or wrote for the London newspapers. In Philadelphia in 1729 Benjamin Franklin took over *The Pennsylvania Gazette*, promising that it would be "an agreeable and useful Entertainment" as well as carrying news and advertisements.

The revenue obtained from advertising made the owning of a newspaper more profitable. Printers such as Franklin had founded newspapers to show off their skills as well as to provide news. Then came the proprietors, whose principal aim was to make money. From the middle of the 18th Century onwards, more and more new titles were launched. In London in 1785 came the best known of them all: *The Times*. It was to set the pattern for newspapers throughout the world.

During the 19th Century other "serious" newspapers were founded which are still being published today: such as *The New York Times* (1851), *The Daily Telegraph* (1855), *The Manchester Guardian* (now *The Guardian*), *The Scotsman*, and *The Age* of Melbourne (1854).

The 19th Century also saw the rise of the "popular press" and of mass circulation. In 1833 James Gordon Bennett, Sr. founded the *New York Herald* after seeing the initial success of the **penny press**. His son succeeded him and expanded circulation even further with sensational stunts, such as sending the journalist Henry Morton Stanley to Africa in search of Dr Livingstone.

In England the national popular press emerged in 1843 with *The News of the World*. This was followed by *Tit-Bits*, to compete with which the Harmsworth brothers began to create their press empire: rescuing the *Evening News* in 1894, and launching the *Daily Mail* in 1896. In 1908 Alfred Harmsworth, later Lord Northcliffe, bought *The Times*.

This painting by David Wilkie shows army veterans at Chelsea in London eagerly reading an account of the Battle of Waterloo in 1815. At that time, newspapers were the public's only source of news.

Linotype setters at work on the London *Daily Mail* in the 1930s. The Linotype machine set type in a single line instead of as individual letters.

Who Makes a Newspaper?

NEWSPAPERS

PROPRIETOR AND BOARD
PUBLISHER

EDITOR

Deputy editor   Managing editor

Local news editor
Copy-editors
Reporters

Political editor
Political correspondents

City editor
Copy-editors
Reporters

Pictures editor
Photographers
Researchers
Dark room

Night editor
Chief copy-editor
Copy-editors

Associate editors
Leader writers

Sports editor
Sports copy-editors
Sports reporters

Art editor
Artists
Designers
Cartoonists

Foreign editor
Foreign copy-editors
Foreign correspondents
Stringers

Features editor
Arts editor
Critics and contributors

Literary editor
Critics and contributors

Fashion editor
Fashion assistant

Features copy-editors
Freelance contributors

Production editor

These two diagrams show the main departments and jobs on a large international newspaper. The Editor and his staff are responsible for all the articles and pictures. The General Manager and his staff are responsible for the production and distribution of the paper.

The Editor is helped by his Deputy, his Associate Editors and his Night Editor who takes over late in the evening. The Managing Editor looks after the administration.

The Home News, Foreign, Features, Sports and City Editors supervise the pages which cover their particular subjects.

The Picture Editor organizes the photographs for the whole paper. The Art Editor is responsible for the overall design and for commissioning all the drawings, cartoons and diagrams.

The Production Editor is the link between the editorial and printing departments.

Under the General Manager, the Production Manager for Pre-press is in charge of processing the articles and pictures ready for printing. The Production Manager for Press is in charge of printing the newspaper. The Circulation Department arranges the delivery of the finished copies.

The Advertisement Department handles all the "ads." The Technical Services Manager looks after the machines and plant.

GENERAL MANAGER

Advertising director

Advertisement manager
Advertising staff

Technical services manager
Technical staff

Production director

Production manager for pre-press
Page layout operators
Color origination staff
Process production staff

Production manager for press
Press supervisor
Print operators

Circulation director

Circulation manager
Circulation staff

Front Page Story

The Times for 20 October 1987

9.30 a.m. London time

On coming in to work, city page staff, market reporters and city editor see big fall on London markets shown on the Topix (official Stock Exchange) system on their computers. A plunge in the US dollar is also evident from the exchange rates.

10.45

Business page conference
Reporters dispatched to investigate the fall and to write it up. One reporter and photographer sent to security dealers (stockbrokers) for on-the-spot color cover.

14.30

London markets plunge. The dollar has dropped again. All awaiting US market opening. US economics correspondent now in office and covering US scene for business news.

Artist commissioned to draw graphic chart. Information is constantly updated on screen. Note how dollar drops right off chart in final steep plunge at 5pm.

Picture desk scanning photographs. Reporters back and writing. Cartoon artist commissioned for cartoon.

20.00

First edition off from copy-editor's desk to photocomposition.

20.30

After Wall Street closes, full extent of US crisis realized. Headline changed. US color stories added in later editions.

12.00

Editor's conference.
London Stock Exchange fall and dollar dive considered for front page lead story.

Leader conference follows immediately. Leader writer starts working on the first version of the leader. He has to rewrite it four times, to keep up with events.

16.00

Editor's conference. US crash now evident. Front page discussed.

18.30

Night staff on. City staff finishing reports.

19.30-20.00

Front page copy to copy-editors who check layout for setting and add headings.

THE TIMES

TUESDAY OCTOBER 20 1987

No 62,904

Dow Jones crashes 508 points: City wipes £50bn off shares

Wall Street's blackest hours

- Share prices on Wall Street plunged by nearly a quarter in one day, a far steeper drop than in the crash of 1929
- In London, the FT-SE 100 share index fell 250 points, cutting more than £50 billion from share values
- The dollar dropped sharply. Mr James Baker, US Treasury Secretary, went into urgent talks with the West German Finance Minister
- British Petroleum shares plunged 34p down at 316p. The Government's offer price is 330p, but the Treasury said the sale would go ahead

By Kenneth Fleet

Yuppies feel the pinch of poverty

From Charles Bremner, New York

BP shares below offer price

By Our City Staff

Crash of '87

Above. Editorial conference at the *Boston Globe* in the 1930s.

Left. James Gordon Bennett Jr. of the *New York Herald* shown in a cartoon of 1884. He became editor when his father, who founded the paper, died in 1872, and he retained control for fifty years. He enjoyed signing up famous writers, such as Mark Twain, and backing sensational stunts.

The Editor

The editor is in charge of the newspaper. He is responsible for everything that appears in it, and his word is final in deciding what should be printed or not.

An editor has three groups of people to consider: the publisher and board of directors who own the paper, the staff who run it, and the readers.

The board needs to be kept informed of what is going on by regular reports, and they are the people who have to be consulted when something out of the ordinary happens.

In the past, some proprietors used their power to dictate the policy of a newspaper, but nowadays a guarantee of independence is usually built in to an editor's contract. Most proprietors want a newspaper to make money, which means that the editor has to sell more copies and to attract more advertising.

On a large daily newspaper, editorial conferences take place twice a day, when the editor meets the heads of the various departments to decide what will go into the paper the following day. The late morning conference is to discuss what is in the **diary**. The late afternoon conference is to discuss how the news is shaping up and to finalize its coverage in the paper—though this is always subject to the inclusion of a last-minute story.

The conferences are attended by the Home News Editor, the Foreign News Editor, the City Editor, the Sports Editor, the Pictures Editor, etc.—altogether about a dozen people. Each briefly describes the stories that they have to offer. The editor may comment or make suggestions. Within their own department, all of

Above. Editorial conference at *The Times* of London, taken by the present editor, Charles Wilson.

Right. Thomas Barnes, editor of *The Times* from 1817 to 1841, from a miniature painted in 1834. He earned the paper the nickname of "The Thunderer" and was reputed to be the most powerful man in Britain.

these page editors are responsible for the contents of their own pages. The conferences enable them to have an overall view of the paper and its contents.

After the morning conference there is a leader-writers' meeting when the editor agrees on subjects for the leading articles. These are important because they express the views of the newspaper and what it stands for.

On a weekly newspaper, conferences take place once or twice a week. On a small local paper there may only be three people on the editorial staff. The purpose is still the same: to discuss the news and how to handle it.

During the day, the editor will see members of his staff individually if he wants to discuss future ideas and projects. He will also see people from outside the newspaper, and will take care to contact and stay in touch with news-makers who are important and active in their own fields.

He keeps up with the news by studying radio and television reports and by watching other papers to see what stories his rivals are producing.

The editor's responsibility is to make his paper the best of its kind: first by reporting the news, with excellent commentary and a flow of new ideas, but always staying true to the character of the newspaper. A newspaper has its own personality, which is familiar to the readers and is their reason for buying it. If a businessman's staid economic journal stops analyzing stocks and shares and starts headlining sex scandals he will give it up and look for another providing reliable financial news. (He may first write to the editor to say what he feels. Letters to the editor are always given careful attention!)

So the good editor always thinks of his readers first and tries to make sure that the newspaper gives them what they expect.

Above. H.M. Stanley, the reporter sent by Gordon Bennett of the *New York Herald* to find Dr Livingstone lost in Africa.
Left. Stanley's famous greeting, "Dr Livingstone I presume", when they finally met.

The Reporter

The reporter gathers and writes the news. The source of the news could be the diary kept by the paper. Or it could come from a news agency, flashed up on the computer screen or clicking in on a tape. It could be a **press release**. Or it could be a telephone tip-off. Whatever the source, the reporter is sent to investigate and report.

The reporter has to be good at getting around, at tracking people down, and at persuading them to talk. Sent to cover a local fire, s/he must first find the scene and then locate the key witness. S/He will need a quick eye for detail and a nose for facts—names, ages, occupations of the witnesses; how, why and where did the fire start? Curiosity and quick action also help: the fire engine seen and followed in the street might lead to a scoop. Most important is the ability to write, to describe what has been seen vividly without wasting words.

Having obtained the story, the reporter has to turn it in. If s/he is back in the office, s/he settles down to the computer or typewriter, heads the copy with an identifying catchphrase, and passes it on to the news desk. If s/he is on **location**, s/he can phone it back to the telephone reporters' room where it will be taken down by specially trained staff who pass it on to the news desk.

On a small local paper, a reporter is expected to cover everything from an agricultural show to an interview with a visiting celebrity. On a larger paper with several reporters, the page editor sends whoever s/he thinks most suited to the story.

Some assignments are short: just half a day's work. Others can last for months.

Reporters based abroad are known as foreign correspondents. They have to be aware of what is happening in their host country, but must still stay in close contact with their foreign news desks at home. Like all other journalists they study the news—from the local papers, radio and television, and from the agency reports which they receive on their computer screens around the world.

Foreign correspondents are accredited as the representatives of their papers and receive invitations to **press conferences**. They build up local contacts. If possible, they rent an office where press facilities are available—with another newspaper or in a press center which has the communications for filing **copy** and pictures and a library to consult.

The foreign editor will send the correspondent, like the reporter, to cover particular stories. He or she will also be asked for local **color** on stories which are running at home and which have an angle concerning the particular country, such as Mafia roots in Italy when a case crops up in America or England.

Foreign correspondents are often expected to cover huge areas. For example, the whole of Europe including the Iron Curtain countries may be covered from London by one person. So they have to be prepared to travel at a moment's notice, in most cases taking with them a lap computer plus modem and adaptor, convertible plug and an adequate supply of batteries.

On arrival at the destination, the first essential item is a telephone to contact the head office for any further instructions and to set up the link for filing copy. Big news agencies have **ports** for computers around the world, so that by dialling a local number, copy can be transmitted instantly to the home paper. Failing that, the correspondent has to improvise another method. S/He could write the most brilliant account of an earthquake, flood or terrorist attack, but unless s/he can deliver it to its destination s/he will be wasting her/his time.

Above. Mrs Thatcher, Prime Minister of Great Britain, briefing reporters at a European Community press conference in Brussels. Some reporters are based in Brussels, regularly covering the Community Parliament for their papers. Others will have been sent out specially for the occasion. Below. The news room of *The Times* in London. Reporters use the computer terminals to write their articles then send them to the central memory to be held with all the articles for their page. They can also call up news agency service reports on the screen to see what is happening around the world.

The Pictures Editor

The pictures editor is responsible for all the photographs that appear in a newspaper. These can be specially taken by the paper's own photographers, be supplied by **picture agencies**, or come from the paper's photo library.

A pictures editor's day begins the night before: watching the television news to see what is happening. If an exciting story breaks, he telephones a photographer and asks him/her to cover it immediately. In the morning he listens to the radio news, as well as reading the papers, always in search of a new idea, an unexpected angle for a picture.

Once in his office, he must decide where to send his photographers. The morning conference tells him how news stories are being handled. If the news editor is dispatching a team on a story, he may send a photographer with them. The features editor will have provided him with a list of portraits and more leisurely subjects needed for any special interviews or articles. There is not the same pressure from features as from hard news.

A national or big regional newspaper has a team of photographers, varying from around six for the more serious papers to around twenty for the popular **tabloids** which illustrate every story and often have more pictures than text. One of the pictures editor's skills lies in the deployment of his team. He has to know their different strong points: some are good at hard news; some are better at sympathetic shots. Apparently unrelated talents—such as being a good, fast driver—can be important when you need to reach the scene in a hurry. When sending out the first photographers, he must make sure that he will not be short later in the day if a story breaks and he needs instant photo coverage.

He will also have a list of photographers around the country and abroad whom he knows he can call on if something happens in their area.

As soon as a photographer has taken his pictures he needs to have them developed and printed, quickly. If he is working with a mobile team which has its own van and developing equipment, the pictures can be processed on the way and sent to the office by wire. Otherwise,

Right. Matthew Brady, photographer of the American Civil War, who took his photographic wagon right up to the front lines.
Above. A Brady picture of General Grant.

a dispatch rider can bring them to the office to be developed in the dark room. The very latest cameras actually have their own processing device which can be attached to a telephone and transmits photographs down the line.

Small **contact prints** are made from each of the rolls of film. The pictures editor selects the best half-dozen from the whole take, to offer to the news editor. In the final selection he will try to include both horizontal and vertical shots, to fit in with either format in the layout.

During the day, the picture agencies are producing their own photographs of the news as it happens. In modern offices these are beamed on to screens so that the pictures editor can see all of them and choose any he wants. Most newspapers have contracts with the picture agencies, as have the news desks for news agency reports. With modern equipment, even television news bulletins can be recorded, the frames frozen, and a transparency made for use as a picture.

As the newspaper takes shape, the page editors will realize that they need "mug shots" of people or places. The pictures editor will ask the paper's photo library, which holds its own old photographs and some from outside sources, to see what they can produce.

A good pictures desk comes from teamwork between the editor, the photographer, the fast dispatch rider, the dark room, and the researchers in the library.

At the picture desk of *The Sunday Times* in London the photographer Sally Soames and the Picture Editor Michael Cranmer look at contact prints of her pictures. A computer screen for showing agency pictures is on the wall behind.

The Specialist

Sports reporters crowd round the quarterback John Elway of the Denver Broncos during the 1988 Superbowl.

The Sports Reporter has to be able to tell what happened in a game, how it happened, and why it happened. He must be an expert on his sport, and must be able to identify every player on the field and to describe not just who scored the goal but who passed to whom so that the goal was scored. He must know the history of the sport, so that when something spectacular occurs he can recognize it. Most important of all, he must be able to rise to the occasion in describing it. He has to remember that he is writing for fellow-experts. His readers will often know as much about their favorite sport as he does, and will probably have been watching the same match. So he has to be able to hold them by the quality of his writing. To be dull is the ultimate sin of the sports reporter. Deadlines rule him. He must be totally reliable, able to watch the end of the match or race, and get his copy in by phone in the half-hour left before the paper goes to press.

The Fashion Editor will have developed an acute awareness and sense of fashion. She goes to the fashion shows in the spring and autumn, especially to Paris, Milan and Spain, and notes the emerging trends in clothes which women will want to wear during the next season. *Prêt-à-porter*—the ready-to-wear collections—and press parties attended by the stylists are as important as *haute couture*. Back at home the fashion editor searches out the designers and shops who are following these trends. They are happy to lend her clothes for a feature because of the publicity it will bring them. She then has to assemble the right models for the latest look, an excellent fashion photographer, and, very important, the accessories and set-up for the shoot in a studio or on location. For some clothes a colorful location is essential—convincing beach shots for swimsuits are difficult in a freezing studio in January—so she also has to be able to come up with ideas for matching the clothes to the locations or to a suitable studio background.

The Gossip Columnist has to be totally familiar with his or her world, whether it is Hollywood stars or the aristocracy in England. S/He needs to know who are friends, who are feuding, who is married to whom, and who has been married to whom. S/He needs an accurate eye for names and faces in order to recognize all these characters. S/He needs physical stamina to be able to attend endless first nights and to tackle the next extravagant party with enthusiasm instead of dropping off to sleep half-way through. S/He also needs the knack of knowing where the action is happening and not being stuck behind a table three rooms away. S/He needs to be able to relay all the gossip to her/his readers in a lively style, not just as a list of names and places.

The Political Correspondent has to read all the official documents issued by the government. These tell her/him what legislation is under consideration. S/He may have to prepare a simpler, more readable version of the documents, to make them clear to the readers. S/He has to keep in close touch with politicians, in order to find out what is happening behind the scenes as well as in the official debates and statements. S/He must be able to deduce when a minister or secretary of state is on the way out of office, and to receive early notice of any new alliance. S/He must be considered trustworthy by politicians. S/He has to attend official debates and must be prepared to write them up, either reporting them exactly as they take place, or in a more colorful way using her/his inside information.

Above. Front-row view for fashion editors from around the world at the Lacroix salon in Paris.

Right. Hedda Hopper (on right), the legendary Hollywood gossip columnist, greeting stars at the British première of the film *Showboat* in 1936.

The Design Department

The design department produces all the **graphics** in the newspaper: that is all the illustrations which are drawings not photographs—such as maps, diagrams, charts, cartoons, and logos used to indicate a special feature.

The subjects for the next day's graphics are agreed upon at the morning conference. The page editor or design director briefs the artist, giving any information s/he has, and specifying the required size. The artist may not work to the exact size, but s/he needs to know the space s/he will have to fill so that the proportions will be correct. A laser camera can then scale the art up or down as necessary.

In order to produce a map, the artist will have to consult the library to find out the basic outline. To indicate different areas s/he can use self-adhesive sheets covered with different patterns which can be cut to the size and shape required. The type is set by the word-processing computer and is pasted down or mechanically added by the laser camera.

A diagram or drawing forms part of the article that it illustrates, giving information which can be understood more easily in visual form than in words. It should fit in with the text, and a good artist will vary his style accordingly. A simple table for the business page only needs a plain, straightforward presentation, but the layout of a police siege should capture some of the tense atmosphere.

On average, an artist working in a newspaper office will produce three or four drawings a day, taking three or four hours to complete each one. If they are not due for the next day's paper, illustrations for features can be produced at a more leisurely pace, and most features departments have some articles with illustrations standing ready.

A cartoonist may work in the newspaper office itself or may prefer her/his own studio. S/He still has to produce a drawing at speed and to deliver it in time to go to press. Cartoonists

An artist at his drawing board preparing a map for the newspaper USA Today.

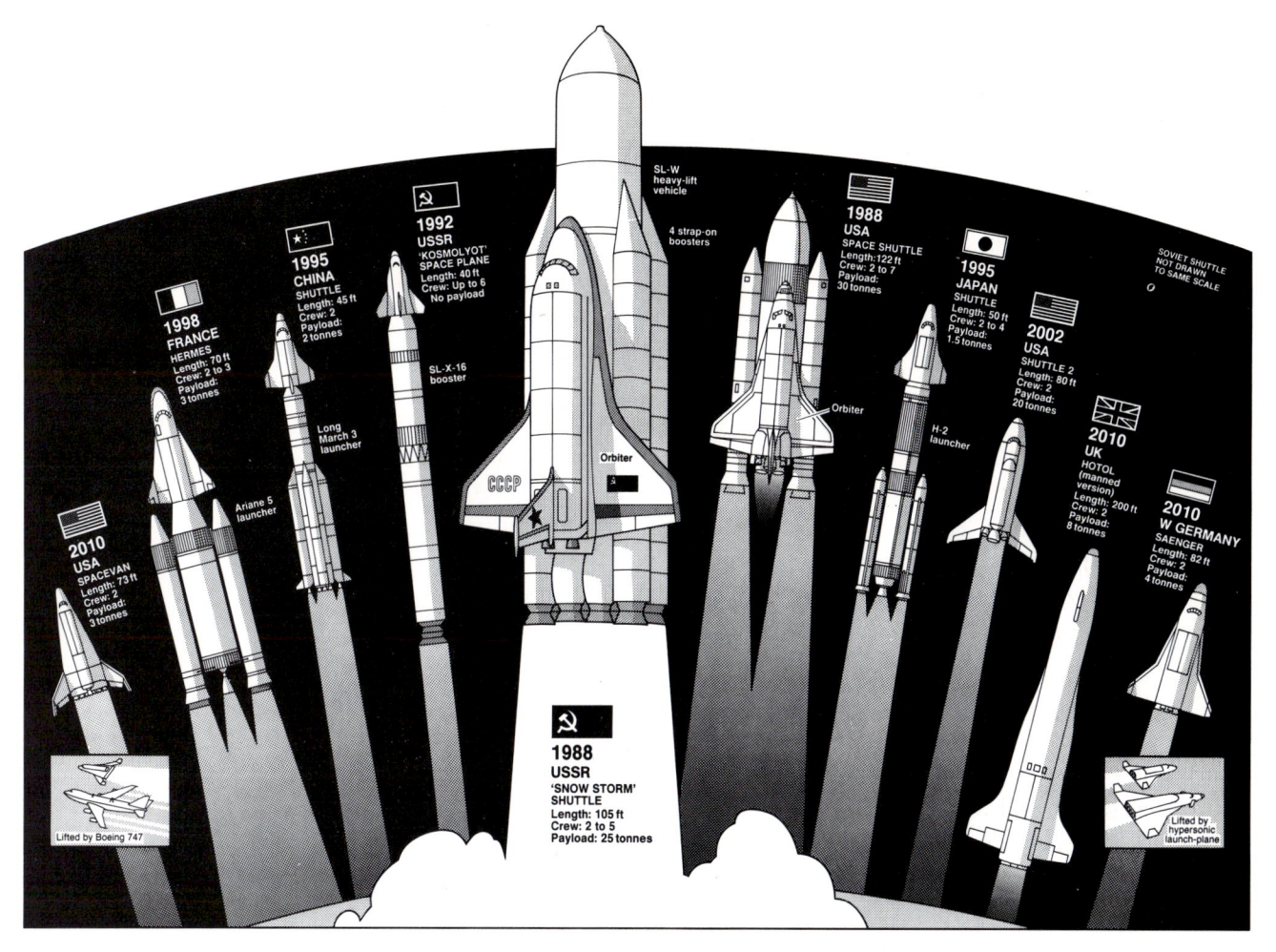

usually develop their own, very recognizable, style. A newspaper will choose a cartoonist because the editor likes her/his style and wants her/his individual commentary on the news or the caricaturist's view of prominent personalities. Cartoonists are usually given a free hand and in some cases may even disagree with the ideas of the editor.

The design department is also responsible for the overall appearance of a newspaper. The news editors lay out the news pages but a designer lays out any feature pages involving pictures and drawings. If an editor wants to give the paper a new look, the department will be asked to produce ideas for **type faces**, sizes, column widths, etc., and a complete visual presentation of the pages.

Diagram of future shapes and sizes of nuclear missiles drawn for *The Times* of London.

Below. Fred Basset began his cartoon career in London's *Daily Mail* 25 years ago. Now the strip runs in all five continents and is translated into every European language.

The Copy-Editor

The copy-editor receives the "raw" copy from the reporter or contributor and turns it into a newspaper item.

The first stage is to check it, thoroughly. S/He checks simple points, such as spelling and grammar (the copy-editor's desk in any newspaper office has a supply of dictionaries and reference books on hand). Using the reference books s/he checks the facts. If s/he is uncertain about something s/he consults the library and makes telephone calls. S/He checks the style of the copy, to see that it is in correct English—and, most important, that it is in the **house style** of the newspaper. On a serious paper this could mean using longer words and sentences. On a tabloid it could mean a more colloquial approach, using snappy sentences with short words.

Then s/he has to make the story fit the space allocated to it on the page. The chief copy-editor or the page editor will have passed her/him the rough **layout**, either as a physical sketch or called up on the computer. The **catchline** at the head of each story will have been roughly shown in its space on the layout with the number of lines that it is to occupy. The copy-editor must make sure that the copy is precisely the required length, including headlines.

These tasks used to be laboriously carried out by counting the words and calculating the space that they would occupy in the chosen type size. With **computer type-setting** it is much simpler. The reporter sends his article with the catchline and page number to the computer memory. The copy-editor types in the catchline and page number to call it up. The computer's software has a **font** of types and sizes. All the copy-editor has to do is to key in the particular type that s/he wants and specify the size and column width. The computer flashes it on the screen and adds up the total number of lines so that s/he knows how much s/he has to cut and how much space is available for **headlines**.

Choosing headlines is an art. The words have to be short to fit the column width. They have to attract attention, first by summing up the whole story then by leading the reader down the column. They must break up the text so that it does not look boring, but without stopping the flow of the story.

Once s/he is satisfied, the copy-editor takes a print-out of the story (which is what journalists call articles) so that s/he and the page editor can read the proof and make any corrections needed. The print-outs are collated and fed back into the computer, and the story is passed for setting.

On some systems, setting means that the story is held in the computer memory with the rest of its page, ready to be put on film all together. This is called computer setting by direct input. On other systems, the computer produces a bromide: a very clear print on shiny paper to the precise size specified. The bromide is pasted on to a ruled outline of the page, known as a **grid**. When all the items are in place on the grid it is photographed. This is called setting by **photocomposition**.

The copy-editors' desk on *USA Today*. Here the articles are called up on the computer screens, checked for style and accuracy, cut to fit the space available on the page and given headlines to catch the reader's eye. Copy-editors often work in shifts through the day and night to keep pace with newspaper printing runs.

Page Make-up

Newspapers generally carry the most important news on the front page, and sports on the back page. A serious paper **leads** with several stories. Popular tabloids often run only one.

There are differing views on either side of the Atlantic as to which is the most eye-catching part of a page. The British believe that the top left-hand corner is where the lead story attracts most attention. Americans favor the top right-hand corner.

As a general rule, the front page is followed by local news, foreign news, and features, in that order. Most people feel that events at home matter more than what is happening abroad, so they want to read about them first. Then they like to be able to browse through the feature articles—gossip columns, personality interviews, fashion, arts, book reviews, sports. As there are many popular sports and a great many sports readers, there are usually several sports pages.

For the convenience of readers, items such

Preparing pictures on a computer graphics system. The pictures have been fed into the memory and are called up on the screen to be adjusted for size and tone so that they will fit their spaces on the page.

as television program times and the crossword puzzle must be easy to find, so they are always in the same place on the same page. Advertisement space is set up early in the day and the editors are given the size details.

The layout of the news pages is decided by the page editor and the chief copy-editor. They draw up roughs—which are sketches with headings scribbled for the stories and spaces left for the copy, pictures and graphics. Each **dummy** is numbered and the items of copy carry the corresponding page number and heading catchline. Picture sizes are marked and each picture is given a reference number.

The **electronic page and make-up operators** transfer the sketch and headings to the computer on the page layout terminal. The reporter and the copy-editor can each call it up from the memory when they are preparing the copy. The layout can be printed out as many times as necessary, to see how it looks. The design can be altered on the screen and printed out again.

Throughout the evening and night, as different news stories break, the page layouts are changed to carry them.

The sketched "rough" for the front page of *Today* for May 25th, 1988. The sketch is keyed in to the central computer memory on an electronic page layout terminal. It is called up by the editors handling the articles for the page so that they can see the overall layout and the space that they have to fill.

The headings at the top give the information to identify it:
Day 3 is Wednesday.
Paper TD is *Today*.
Edn 1 is first edition.
Sect A is Section A.
Page 1 is the front page.
Copy A is the original copy.
Date 2505 is May 25th.

Processing

Once the night editor has approved a page layout he telephones down to the process department to stand by to receive it. An operator loads a film in its cartridge into the **image setter**. The machine reads the page from the computer memory and burns the image with a laser beam on to the film. The operator takes the film in its cartridge from the image setter to the processor. He links the film edge to the first roller and it goes through a series of processes: developing, fixing and drying—as with an ordinary film.

Meanwhile the photographs and artwork have been sent down by the pictures editor, marked with their page, catchline, captions and reference numbers and with any **cropping** instructions on the back. The operator **keys** the identification to the computer. He puts the pictures on the **densitometer** for measuring light and dark, and then feeds them into the **flat bed laser scanner**, programming it with the special instructions which ensure that the pictures will be correctly scanned. They are flashed up on screen for cropping. The operator can adjust the cropping lines on the screen, as with a computer game.

When a batch of pictures is ready, the operator sends them as digitized information to the central computer memory. As the page is processed by the image setter, the pictures are called up automatically from the memory into their correct position on the layout and they also appear on the film. The only spaces now left are for color.

The next stage is to join the pages which are to be printed together. This is done by the planners, using grids. When they are together they are called strippers. Each stripper has holes punched in it to line up on the grid. It is then taped down. In the planning room a copy-editor checks the text.

The strippers are placed in exposure frames on **light-sensitive film**. The front is drawn down, like a blind. A light is turned on, and the image is now on the film.

The film is taken to a facsimile (fax) machine which transmits it to the printers. A pair of pages is placed on a grid set in the front of the machine. On a special telephone line, the operator phones the **print centers** and tells them that the pages are coming. He presses a button and the page is sucked on to a drum inside the machine. A laser beam scans the information on the pages, converts it into digitized information, and sends it down the special line to the print centers.

Color pictures are taped, one at a time, on to a glass cylinder. They are scanned by a laser beam which travels down the drum. It converts the pictures into digitized information and separates the four primary colors. The information is stored in the computer memory.

On a color-planning table the operator lines the color slots in the layouts on to a grid. He calls the pictures up on a **color monitor** and superimposes the color slot frame on to the picture on the screen. He positions it, sizes it, and crops it as necessary to fit the format. On the same machine he can change the colors of the picture, retouch it, add items by freehand, and take out anything not wanted—such as bloodshot eyes or uneven skin tones.

All the instructions are keyed into the computer memory and the picture is sent, as digitized information, to the print center. It is transmitted four times for its four separate colors. The four colors are cyan (blue), magenta (red), yellow, and black. Any black text accompanying the picture is added to the black separation.

Right. Diagram showing how newspaper pages are paired together for printing.

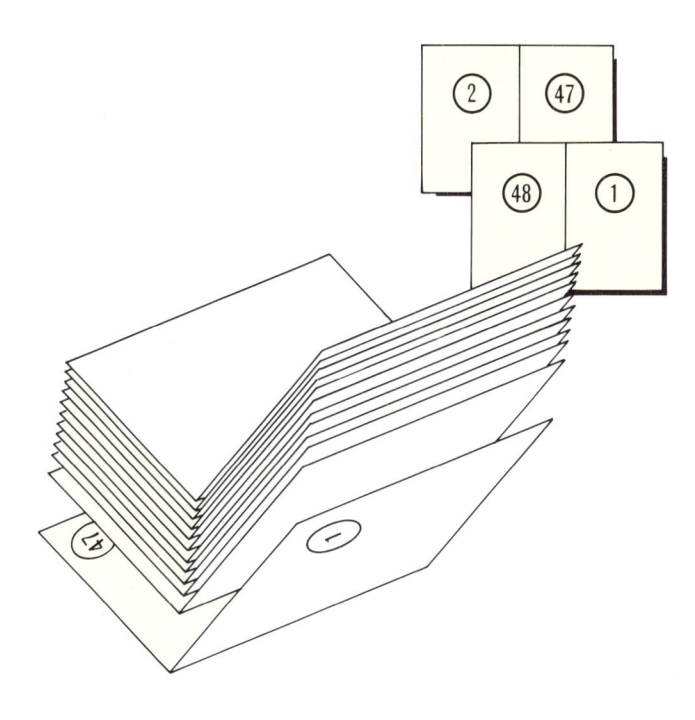

Two more stages in producing the front page of *Today* for May 25th, 1988:

Left. The page developed from the image setter film. It includes text and black and white pictures.

Right. The final front page. The color has been added to the photograph of Michael Jackson and the blue background to the title. The black and white text in these areas was printed at the same time.

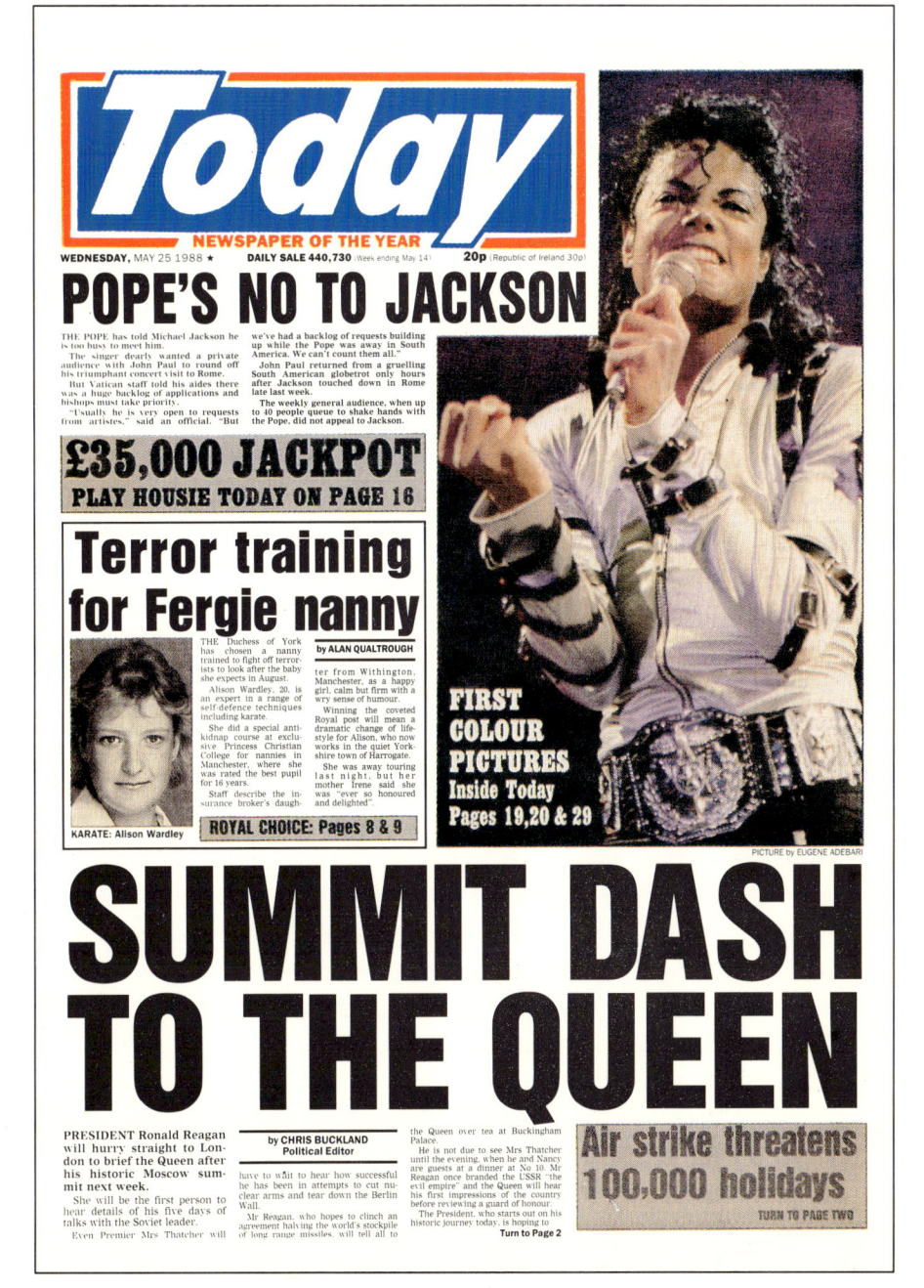

25

Printing and Publishing

A newspaper is printed and packaged for distribution in a single operation at a print center or production department.

The first stage is plate-making. A laser scanner receives the digitized information from the processing scanner for the two pages or stripper. It decodes the information and imposes it as a positive image on to a negative film. The film is placed on a computerized light box. An aluminum plate with a light-sensitive coating is put on top of it, exposed to ultra-violet light and developed. The plate now carries the image of the pages. It is bent at the ends in a machine to make it fit on to the press, and is then set in place on the **plate cylinders**.

The method of printing used by most modern newspapers is called web offset. The web is the paper, which comes in huge rolls of 3 sizes: 64 ins (1600mm), 48ins (1200mm), or 32ins (800mm), used according to the number of pages in the newspaper. A big roll weighs about 2205lbs (1000 kilos). They are delivered by truck and handled by clamp trucks, which resemble fork-lifts, with giant flipper-like clamps to grip the rolls.

The rolls are transferred to a reel stand, which feeds the printing press in a continuous stream, or web. Each stand has three reels. One feeds a roll of paper up to the press; one is loaded, ready to take over; and one is empty, waiting for the next roll. Each roll has double-sided sticky tape on the outside. As one roll nears its end, the next reel moves closer and closer, revolving at the same speed until suddenly the paper is caught up by the sticky tape and joined to the outgoing roll. It takes over smoothly without stopping production.

Automatic cutters chop the old roll and the reel drops back for reloading.

When the paper reaches the printing presses it travels over the inking rollers and then through the blanket cylinders which carry the image and print it on to the paper. Offset printing is based on the chemical reaction of oil in the ink and water on the printing plates fitted with the pages. The plate puts the image on to a thick piece of material called a blanket and the paper takes it off the blanket. So the printing is not direct but offset via the blanket.

The ink is kept in huge drums, some as big as twenty tons, and is pumped from the tanks to the presses. The level of ink is computer controlled. The printing, whether in black and white or in color, is always laid on the paper in dots. The mixture of dots determines the color. Fewer black dots look grey. Blue and yellow dots together look green.

The printed paper travels on, still as a continuous stream, to the folder. This machine slices it into the separate sheets, folds them together in order and newspapers emerge. They pour out on to a conveyor-belt. Fast presses produce 60,000 copies an hour. Production operators are constantly scrutinizing the newspapers at this point, picking out random samples to check the color and quality of the printing.

The conveyor-belt carries the papers to the mail rooms, where a machine stacks them into bundles of twenty-four (**quires**), laying them alternate ways to keep them level. In their bundles they travel on down the conveyor-belt to be tied with plastic strapping ready for delivery.

Above. Print operator changing the plate on a cylinder in a printing unit. Updated news has resulted in a page being altered, and a new plate has been made to replace the old one.

Opposite. The printing press of a modern newspaper. The paper rolls can just be seen on the floor below (bottom left of picture). The paper travels up in a continuous web over the rollers in the printing units, into the folder, where it is cut and folded. The finished newspapers are then taken on the conveyor belt to be packaged in bundles.

Right. Checking the quality of the printing. During the print run, the copies are constantly checked as they come from the folder so that any faults can be detected at once and put right.

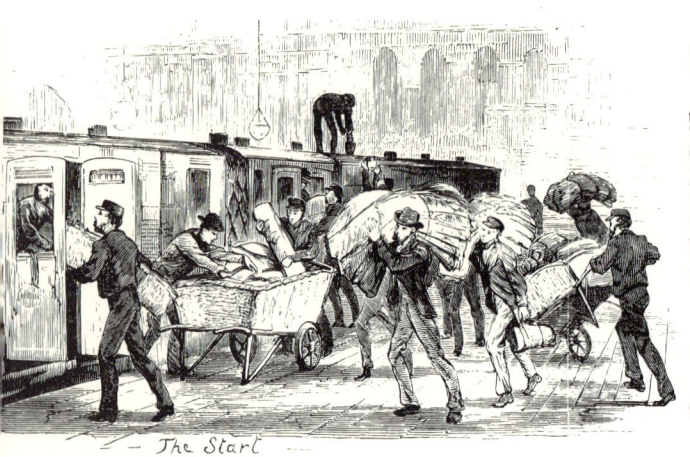

Distribution and Sales

Once the newspapers have been printed they must be dispatched to various distribution points throughout the country. At the printing plant huge trucks wait in long lines to receive the papers in **trunks** as they come off the presses.

The papers are packed in bundles, color-coded to show their edition and destination. They are either built up in the trailers—in the same way as a brick wall is built, but with giant bundles instead of bricks—so that they are packed solid and will not move in transit; or they are pre-loaded on wooden pallets which are hoisted on to the trailers by fork-lift trucks.

The process of distribution goes on all through the night, with relays of trucks coming to load up the different editions. They arrive at about 10pm to collect the papers which will be going the furthest distances, but it is not until the small hours that the latest editions are driven off to be delivered in the nearest districts.

From the plant, the trucks carry the papers either to the nearest railway station or to pick-up points in different parts of the country. The pick-up points are vast warehouses where wholesalers collect the bundles to distribute them to the retailers.

A typical wholesaler will send ten to fifteen vans to pick up the bundles. Each van driver takes the correct number of bundles for his area and breaks them up into the titles and numbers for the retail shops on his run. The van speeds around its district, dropping off the orders to all the shops, from large newsagents to small corner stores.

The retailer has to start work at 5 o'clock in the morning, when the newspapers are

Distribution in 1989. Above. Newspapers strapped ready for delivery.

Right. Loading papers into the "trunk", the body of the huge truck which will deliver them by road around the country. Each trunk can carry over 100,000 papers, which arrive down the spiral on the conveyor belt on the left. They have to be packed carefully and solidly so that they do not move and get damaged during the journey.

delivered. He checks the numbers against his regular order and sorts them out again, putting some on display by his counter and marking others with local addresses.

At 6 o'clock the first newsboys and newsgirls come to collect their papers—stowing them in their bags and taking them out on their delivery rounds.

Papers to be dispatched overseas are taken direct to the nearest airport or to an air carrier who will deal with Customs. Newspapers have to be strapped in the hold of the airplane so that they will not shift around and upset the weight balance.

How newspapers were distributed in England in 1875.

Facts and Figures

Some great newspapers from round the world

Australia
The Age of Melbourne, founded 1854,
 circulation 510,567 weekdays; 802,892 Sundays
The Australian, f. 1964,
 circ. 135,000 weekdays; 270,000 weekends
The Sydney Morning Herald, f. 1831,
 circ. 260,000
Canada
The (Toronto) Globe and Mail, f. 1844,
 circ. 318,300
The Toronto Star, f. 1892,
 circ. 500,000 weekdays; 800,000 Saturdays
Denmark
Berlingske Tidende, f. 1749,
 circ. 146,685
Eire
The Irish Times, f. 1856,
 circ. 87,000
France
Le Figaro, f. 1826,
 circ. 400,000 weekdays; 700,000 Saturdays
Le Monde, f. 1944,
 circ. 555,403
Germany
Frankfurter Allgemeine Zeitung, f. 1898,
 circ. 341,977 weekdays; 416,957 Saturdays
Die Zeit, f. 1946,
 circ. 400,000
Great Britain
The Daily Mail, f. 1896,
 circ. 1,759,455
The Daily Telegraph, f. 1855,
 circ. 1,146,917
The Guardian, f. 1821,
 circ. 493,582
The Independent, f. 1986,
 circ. 400,355
The Sunday Times, f. 1822,
 circ. 1,300,000
The Times, f. 1785,
 circ. 440,000
Holland
De Telegraaf, f. 1893,
 circ. 702,000
Italy
La Stampa, f. 1867,
 circ. 514,091
Japan
Asahi Shimbun, f. 1888,
 circ. 7,590,987 mornings; 4,608,507 evenings
Norway
Aftenposten, f. 1860,
 circ. 248,248 weekdays; 313045 Saturdays
Spain
El Pais, f. 1976,
 circ. 453,793 weekdays; 776,467 Sundays
Sweden
Dagens Nyheter, f. 1864,
 circ. 400,323
Switzerland
Die Weltwoche, f. 1933,
 circ. 98,501

USA
USA Today (the country's only nationwide daily newspaper) f. 1980,
 circ. 1,500,000 weekdays only.
The Boston Globe, f. 1872,
 circ. 510,567 weekdays; 802,892 Sundays
The Los Angeles Times, f. 1881,
 circ. 1,064,392
The New York Times, f. 1851,
 circ. 1,001,694
The Wall Street Journal, f. 1889,
 circ. 1,917,137
The Washington Post, f. 1877,
 circ. 768,288

Important dates in printing

868 In China a book was printed from carved blocks of wood. A block was carved for each page.
1450s Letterpress printing introduced in Europe, invented by Johann Gutenberg of Mainz, Germany. Each letter was set in place by hand. Early presses were flat and could produce about 100 copies an hour, later increased to about 250 copies an hour.
1476 William Caxton started the first press in England at Westminster.
1638 Stephen Day and his son Matthew started first press in America at Cambridge, Mass.
1814 *The Times* of London introduced a steam-driven press with a revolving cylinder. Production rose to 1,100 copies an hour.
1846 Robert Hoe of New York City built a new revolving press (known as the "lightning press"). It was swiftly adopted by American and British newspapers. Output varied from 2,000 to 8,000 copies an hour.
1866 John Walter III of *The Times* of London patented a new press capable of printing both sides of the sheet from a continuous reel of paper. Output 10,500 copies an hour.
1886 The *New York Tribune* introduced setting by linotype machine, which enabled lines to be set for printing instead of each letter being placed by hand. The line of type was called a "slug".
1962 Photocomposition from line-casting computer tapes introduced at *The Los Angeles Times*.
1971 Computer setting with direct "front-end system" introduced by the *Scottish Daily Record* and the *News Journal*, Daytona Beach, Florida.
1985 Computer setting with direct front-end system introduced nationally in Britain on the new newspaper *Today*.
1986 Simultaneous printing of *Asahi Shimbun* in Japan, Los Angeles, New York and London, by satellite transmission.

Miscellaneous

Oldest
A news pamphlet published in Cologne, West Germany in 1470.

Biggest
The Sunday *New York Times* weighed 14lbs (6.35kg) in August 1987.

Highest Circulation
Yomiuri Shimbun in Japan with 14,474,573 copies of its various editions sold on April 1st, 1988.

Longest running strip cartoon
Katzenjammer Kids (Hans and Fritz) first published in *New York Journal*, 1897.

Most syndicated columnist
The letter column of American "agony aunt" Ann Landers has appeared in more than 1200 newspapers.

Glossary

Broadsheet Originally a large sheet of paper printed with news. Now any newspaper with large pages.
Bulletin (news) News broadcast on radio or television.
Catchline Word/s at top of a newspaper article to identify it for page layout.
Clamp truck Small truck used at print center. It has clamps which grip rolls of paper.
Color (in story) Local details and background which enliven an article.
Color monitor Computer screen on which color pictures can be called up and adjusted.
Computer typesetting The modem method of transferring marked-up copy from keyboard to printer.
Contact prints Set of small prints which shows every frame of a roll of film on a single sheet. From these contacts, enlargements are chosen.
Copy The original text of a newspaper article.
Coranto Early form of newspaper.
Cropping Altering size or shape of a photograph by cutting out parts of it.
Diary (In the) Large journal kept by news desk in which events to be covered are listed.
Dummy Sketch of page to show how stories and pictures will be "laid out" (arranged) on the page.
Electronic page layout Computer system for organizing how stories and pictures are laid out.
Flat bed laser scanner Machine in which pictures are placed flat to be scanned by laser so that their details can be fed to the central computer.
Fount (font) Complete assortment of type of the same face, including upper and lower case, and all sizes.
Graphics Any drawn illustrations, such as cartoons, diagrams or logos.
Grid Framework of the exact dimensions of a newspaper.
Headlines Words in large type at the top of an article to catch the eye and give the gist of the story.
House style The kind of story, layout, design, and even spelling, of a particular newspaper.
Image setter Machine which sets images of newspaper articles sent by the computer on to photographic paper.
Key, to To mark position on layout for something to be printed.
Laser scanner Machine which scans picture by laser and transmits the details to the central computer.
Layout The overall design of a newspaper page, showing how the articles and pictures will appear.

Leader Article expressing the opinion of a newspaper. It appears on the same page every day.
Light-sensitive film Film which is affected by being exposed to light.
Mug shot Photo of someone's face.
News-monger Person who gathers news in order to sell it.
On location Working away from home base: e.g. at the scene of an event.
Paste-up Arrangement of proofs of articles, photos, etc., pasted on to sheet before photographing for printing.
Penny press Popular newspapers.
Photocomposition Method of computer typesetting where the computer produces photographic prints as proofs of articles ready for paste-up.
Picture agency Agency supplying pictures.
Plate cylinders Rollers in the printing machines which carry the plates bearing the image of the pages to be printed.
Port (Computer) Point of entry by which information can pass from one end to the other of a computer network.
Press Collective name for newspapers, magazines, etc., as in "The American Press".
Press conference Meeting called so that important person can be interviewed by the press.
Press release Statement circulated for press use.
Print center Place where newspaper printing is carried out.
Print run Number of copies printed at any one time.
Quire 24 copies.
Raw copy Unedited text of an article.
Run, print See *Print run* above.
Run, delivery Journey to deliver (newspapers).
Slug Line of type in linotype setting.
Stone Table on which newspaper is typeset.
Story Newspaper article.
Stylist Person who chooses clothes, accessories and models for a fashion photograph.
Tabloid Newspaper with small size pages, usually for mass circulation.
Trunk Body of truck which carries newspapers.
Typeface A particular shape and design of type, such as "Times", "Baskerville", or "Optima".

Index

Barnes, Thomas 11
Blanket 26
Boston Globe, The 3, 10, 30
Boston Herald, The 3
Boston News-Letter, The 4
Brady, Matthew 14
Bromide 21

Campbell, John 4
Cartoonist 6, 8, 18, 19
Clamp Trucks 26
Corantos/Courantos 4
Cranmer, Michael 15

Daily Courant, The 4
Daily Mail, The 5, 19, 30
Daily Telegraph, The 5
Defoe, Daniel 4
Direct input 21
Dispatch rider 15

Evening News 5

Feature 2, 22
Fielding, Henry 4
Fleet Street 4
Folder 26, 27
Foreign correspondents 12, 13
Franklin, Benjamin 4, 5

Garavi Gujarat 2
Gordon Bennett, James Jr. 5, 10, 12
Gordon Bennett, James Sr. 5, 10

Harmsworth brothers 5

International Herald Tribune, The 2

Lacroix salon 17
Laser camera 18
Letters to the Editor 11
Linotype 5, 30
Livingstone, Dr. 5, 12

Mass circulation 5

New England Courant, The 4
New York Herald 5, 10, 12
New York Times, The 2, 3, 5, 30, 31
News agency 12, 13, 15
News desk 12, 15
News of the World, The 5
News pamphlet 4, 31
News-book 4

Page layout terminal 23
Pennsylvania Gazette, The 4
Photo library 14, 15

Plate-making 26
Popular press 5
Printing press 26, 27, 30

Reel stand 26
Roughs 23

Scotsman, The 5
Soames, Sally 15
Stanley, Henry Morton 5, 12
Strippers 24
Swift, Jonathan 4

Telephone reporters' room 12
"The Thunderer" 11
Times, The 2, 5, 8, 11, 13, 19, 30, 32
Tit-Bits 5
Today 23, 25, 30, 32

USA Today 18, 21, 30

Walter, John 2, 30
Web Offset 26
Weekly Newes from Italy, Germanie, Hungary 4
Wichinaga Gazette, The 2
Wilson, Charles 11

Yomiuri Shimbun, The 3, 31

Acknowledgments

Threshold Books and the publishers are most grateful for the help, advice and cooperation of *The Sunday Times*, *The Times* and *Today* newspapers in the preparation of this book.

Illustration credits
Ace Photo Agency 2; Allsport/Mike Powell 16; BBC Hulton Picture Library 14; Boston Globe 10; the Trustees of the British Library 4 (left); Geoffrey Drury 3 (left), 28 (bottom), courtesy of *Today*; Mary Evans Picture Library 28 and 29 (top); Garavi Gujarat Publications 3 (right); Illustrated London News 17 (bottom); Niall McInerney 17 (top); Mail Newspapers plc 5 (bottom), 19 (bottom); M.A.N. Roland printing press 26; Mansell Collection 10 (inset), 12; Monotype Corporation 22; Rex Features/Bocion, SIPA Press 13 (top); *The Times* 19 (top), *The Times*/Ros Drinkwater front cover, 11, 13 (bottom), 27 (top), 28 (bottom); Times Newspapers 11 (inset), 29 (bottom); *Today* 23, 24, 25 (bottom); *USA Today* 18, 20; Board of Trustees of the Victoria and Albert Museum 5 (top).

Diagrams and drawings: Coral Mula 6, 7, 8; Eddie Poulton 25.

Picture research: Sarah Waters.

How Newspapers Are Made
Copyright © 1989 by Threshold Books Limited, 661 Fulham Road, London SW6 5PZ.

All rights reserved. No part of this book may be reproduced or utilized in any form or by any means, electronic or mechanical, including photocopying, recording, or by any information storage and retrieval systems, without permission in writing from the publisher. For information contact:

Facts On File, Inc.
460 Park Avenue South
New York NY 10016
USA

Library of Congress Cataloging-in-Publication Data
Waters, Sarah.
  How newspapers are made/text, Sarah Waters; design, Eddie Poulton.
  32 p. 30 × 21 cm. (How it is made).
  Includes index.
  Summary: Details different types of newspapers and methods of newspaper production, throughout history and in modern times.
  ISBN 0-8180-2042-6.
  1. Newspaper publishing—Juvenile literature. 2. Journalism—Technique—Juvenile literature. [1. Newspaper publishing.
2. Journalism.] I. Poulton, Eddie. II. Title. III. Series.
PN4734.W35   1989
070.4—dc20   89-31331 CIP AC

Facts On File books are available at special discounts when purchased in bulk quantities for businesses, associations, institutions or sales promotion. Please contact the Special Sales Department of our New York office at 212/683-2244 (dial 800/322-8755 except in NY, AK or HI).

General Editor: Barbara Cooper.
Design by Eddie Poulton.
Composition by Rapid Communications Ltd, London, England.
Printed in England by Maclehose & Partners, Portsmouth.

10 9 8 7 6 5 4 3 2 1

KELLY LIBRARY
EMORY & HENRY COLLEGE
EMORY, VA 24327

3 1836 0014 7629 0